# COLLECTED POEMS

CHARLOTTE MEW

# Collected Poems

*of*

CHARLOTTE MEW

GERALD DUCKWORTH & CO. LTD
3 Henrietta Street, London, W.C.2

*Printed in Great Britain by*
UNWIN BROTHERS LTD. WOKING AND LONDON

# CONTENTS

# CONTENTS

# CHARLOTTE MEW—A MEMOIR

### by ALIDA MONRO

MANY years ago, buying, as was my custom, a copy of *The Nation* one Saturday morning, I opened it eagerly to see if there might be a poem, and was electrified to find printed there "The Farmer's Bride". This poem I immediately committed to memory, and a year or two later repeated it with enthusiasm to Harold Monro, who had recently opened the Poetry Bookshop, with the avowed intention of publishing the work of young poets and presenting them to a large audience.

At his suggestion a letter was written to Charlotte Mew in care of *The Nation*, asking whether or not she had other poems, or a number of poems that could be got together to form a book. Charlotte Mew responded very kindly to the tentative suggestion, but with her characteristic lack of confidence declared that no one would want to read them if they were published. However, she sent another poem, "The Changeling", which, she remarked, might or might not be liked as much as "The Farmer's Bride". This poem also made an immediate impression, and I wrote to her saying that I proposed to read both the poems at the Bookshop on a Tuesday or Thursday evening, on which days there were always readings of poetry at six o'clock in the evening. Charlotte Mew was told that there would also be a number of other interesting new poems read and was asked whether she would care to be present. She replied that she would do her best to be there.

So on that Tuesday evening in far away November 1915 Charlotte Mew came to the Poetry Bookshop for the first time. Let me try to describe her. The Bookshop itself was a small room about twelve feet square, lined from floor to ceiling with books, and opening on to a dark slummy street off Theobald's Road in Bloomsbury. There would be a number of people wandering about looking at the shelves before going up to the reading room. The reading room itself was a converted workroom that had been originally used by the gold-beaters who occupied a large part of the street: and the gentle thud, thud, of their gold-beating hammers rang in the ears of all those who lived there, from morning to night, every day. At about five minutes to six the swing-door of the shop was pushed open and into the room stalked Charlotte Mew. Such a word best describes her walk. She was very small, only about four feet ten inches, very slight, with square shoulders and tiny hands and feet. She always wore a long double-breasted top-coat of tweed with a velvet collar inset. She usually carried a horn-handled umbrella, unrolled, under her arm, as if it were psychologically necessary to her, a weapon against the world. She had very fine white hair that showed traces of once having been a warm brown. Her eyes were a very dark grey, bright with black lashes and highly arched dark eyebrows. Her face was a fine oval, and she always wore a little hard felt pork-pie hat put on very straight. The whole time she was speaking she kept her head cocked at a defiant angle. When she came into the shop she was asked: "Are you Charlotte Mew?" and her reply, delivered characteristically with a slight smile of amusement, was: "I am sorry to say I am". She invariably adopted this self-depreciatory manner when meeting strangers, and invariably spoke as if those who addressed her expected her to defy them. As she got accustomed to a person this defiance vanished completely, and no one could be more warm-hearted and witty in her talk and in her friendship. After that evening at the Poetry Bookshop a close friendship sprang up between us.

When I met her, Charlotte Mew lived in a tall, typically Bloomsbury house, No. 9, Gordon Street, Gordon Square (destroyed by bombs in 1940–41). It was tall and narrow, dark and gaunt inside. She was born on November 15, 1869, at 10, Doughty Street, Mecklenburgh Square, W.C., as were her sisters and brother. They moved to Gordon Street while she was still a child and here she lived for almost her entire life. Her father had been an architect, and the rooms and passages were lined with drawings and plans of his work. He was the son of a yeoman farmer in the Isle of Wight; after coming to London to be articled to an architect, as is often the way with country boys he married his boss's daughter. Charlotte's maternal grandfather, H. E. Kendall (born March 1776 died January 1875) was for fifty years surveyor of St. Martin-in-the-Fields, and was responsible for many buildings in and about the

London area. Her father, Fred Mew (born March 14, 1832, died September 12, 1898), seems to have been a man who took his responsibilities very lightly. His daughter's account of her early life was one of gaiety and extravagance which she enjoyed to the full. However, he died when she was about twenty-nine, leaving nothing, having spent all his available capital on living.

This sudden drop in her financial circumstances had a most damaging psychological effect. Charlotte Mew inherited from her mother a view of life that was very prevalent during the last century, namely that appearances must be kept up at all costs. When I first knew Charlotte, the top half of their house was let to some people, but it was a long time before this was disclosed to me in confidence, as it was felt that such a circumstance was a matter of which to be deeply ashamed. Her mother, whom she addressed as "Ma", was treated very much as if she were a naughty child, and on the evenings that I went there she was always told to go up to bed. Charlotte would always say, when speaking of her mother, that family ties meant everything to her; but it is probable that she adored the idea of a mother rather than the woman herself, for there was little in common between them. "Ma" was a tiny woman, scarcely more than four feet, very shrivelled and with tiny claw-like hands. There was a portrait of her painted in oils hanging on the wall, which showed that in her youth she had been very pretty and bright, like a little bird. She was the mother of four children, a son and three daughters. Charlotte was the eldest girl, then came Anne, her inseparable companion. I never met the youngest sister or the brother, and only after Charlotte's death did I hear from an intimate friend that they had gone out of their minds many years before and were both in asylums. The friend who spoke of them, told me that the third sister, Freda, was as remarkable as the other two and was "like a flame". Their sad condition was a constant torment to Charlotte.

Anne was a little taller than Charlotte, much gayer and much less weighed down by the sorrows of their lives. These lay heavily on Charlotte, whose temperament was naturally keyed very low. Anne bore a striking resemblance to Marie Antoinette. She had the most brilliant violet-blue eyes that I have ever seen, and although she was very fragile and delicate, she always managed to be bright and witty. She was an accomplished artist in redecorating seventeenth-century furniture. She worked all her life painting flowers and fire-screens and renovating

English painted furniture for a firm of antique dealers, who, according to Charlotte, paid her only a sweated wage. Both of them by their upbringing were quite incapable of demanding more, principally, I think, because Anne feared that by making such a demand she would lose the work and thus the money which was badly needed to keep things going.

It must not be thought, as has been supposed by many who judge from Charlotte's own writings, that she was always in a state of depression. This was far from the truth. She was a great teller of stories and always had new ones, never failed to see the humour in any situation, and never went on a visit anywhere without coming back with a riotous account of what had taken place. In her earlier days, while her father was alive and money was plentiful, she made several sojourns in northern France, and always had a great nostalgia for that country. She read French fluently and introduced many interesting books to her acquaintances. She always had a French book going at the same time as an English one and was an indefatigable reader. She also liked playing the organ and had a delicate touch on the piano.

She had one companion in her house—a parrot, Willie, who was said to be at least ninety years old and might have been older. He was a very noisy bird and made great difficulties at her tea parties when he took a dislike to some guest, usually a man, and would not be silenced. She and Anne had an enormous affection for this bird, and when he was ill, as he often was in his later years, Charlotte would frequent the parrot house at the Zoo any moment of the day, and sometimes at night if she could knock up the parrot man, to get help for him. However, as time went on his foot became worse and worse until he could not stand on his perch, and there came a day when I was summoned by Charlotte and told that the parrot man had said that Willie must be put to sleep and that I was the person to do it, as he could not stand men and a veterinary surgeon was therefore out of the question. It was a terrible moment when I was led by the two sisters to a room at the back of the house in complete darkness except for a candle, given a sponge, a large bottle of chloroform and several big blankets, and told that the chloroform was to be put on the sponge, the sponge put into the cage, and the blankets tucked well round to cut off all air so that Willie might be anaesthetised and die. This was done, and the dreary procession of three went downstairs to wait the period prescribed by the chemist as necessary to ensure his death. At the given time I went upstairs, took off the blankets, and put in my hand in the dark to remove the corpse from the floor of the cage, only to receive a smart nip on the finger which nearly caused me to scream hysterically. However, I decided that the two sisters could stand no more, and bravely put in a hand, took the parrot by his neck—he was very weak—and held it till he was dead. I then placed the corpse in the little box waiting to receive him, and went downstairs to report that all was over.

This death fortunately occurred just at the time that the lease of Gordon Street was up and other rooms had to be found to which Charlotte's mother could be removed and which would not be so small as to cause her distress in giving up what had been quite a large house with spacious rooms. The house found was in Delancey Street, Regent's Park, overlooking its green trees. They had the upper part of the house, and Charlotte deplored that two-thirds of their income had to go on paying this rent so that Ma need not feel her lowered social position, which had not been so apparent in Gordon Street where part of the expenses were paid by lodgers. Mrs. Mew did not live very long after the move, and Charlotte then decided to go and camp with her sister in a studio which Anne had always had for her work, but where neither of them had ever thought of living before. This studio was in Hogarth Studios, next door to the Scala Theatre in Charlotte Street. Often in the past Charlotte and Anne had received friends there if they did not want to have them at their home at tea time; but after they went to live there, although it was only a temporary measure, Charlotte decided that no one could possibly be asked to visit. They did not continue this arrangement very long; Anne went and stayed with a great friend in West Hampstead and in various other places until they could decide what to do. However, quite soon Anne, who had always been very delicate and suffered with backache to a terrible degree, suddenly became very much worse. A specialist told her that she had a serious disease for which there was no cure, and in about six months she died.

Charlotte was so overcome by Anne's death that she was inconsolable, and after a short time her nerves became very bad. She was unable to sleep, and so tortured herself with the idea that as she had not had a vein opened in Anne's wrist her sister might have been buried alive, that medical help had to be sought. As a result she went into a nursing home in Beaumont Street for a rest and medical supervision. It was a house with no outlook. She had a bedroom at the back looking on to a high brick wall, and the last time I saw her there she pointed to this wall, on which an occasional pigeon perched, and said how very depressed she felt gazing on to the grey bricks where no sun seemed to come. She went to a miserable chest-of-drawers in the room and took out a copy of her poem "Fin de Fête" which had been transcribed by Thomas Hardy in his own hand and which had lately become one of her most prized possessions. She handed the poem to me saying she would like me to have it, and I took it, feeling rather sad, but not knowing that I would never see her again.

The next morning, March 24, 1928, she went out and bought a bottle of disinfectant and went back and swallowed it. In a brief moment of consciousness when doctors were trying to revive her, she said: "Don't keep me, let me go". It is melancholy to think that when her death was reported in the local Marylebone newspaper, she was casually described as "Charlotte New, said to be a writer".

Charlotte Mew was greatly influenced all her life by her friendships and by her emotional contacts. Perhaps the first and greatest emotional influence in her life was that of her old nurse who cared for her right up to the time of her death when Charlotte was in her twenties. This old nurse died in March 1893 after running her needle into her hand, and a brass memorial was put up to her memory in St. Pancras Church. Charlotte wrote a masterly and moving account of this old woman in *The Nation*. This story is most revealing and shows Charlotte Mew at her very best in her understanding of character.

Charlotte Mew was educated at the Lucy Harrison School for Girls in Gower Street, and for many years helped with Miss Paget's Girls' Club, work which she enjoyed enormously.

She herself was very much two people, though she was unaware of it. She had a strict moral code in respect of other people's conduct, particularly in regard to their sex relationships, and absolutely cut out from her friendship anyone on whom a breath of scandal blew. Readers of "Madeleine in Church" know how well she understood the difficulties of conducting a life on the strait and narrow path in the face of a great and overwhelming emotion. She herself was fully aware of this and I think was the most sincere person one could meet. She never humbugged herself and she hated humbug in others, but she did not like her friends to stray from the path. Some of her contemporaries have told me that they always expected that she might find rest and consolation in the

Catholic Church, and she was, as her poems show, very much possessed by the idea of Christ and the Cross, though it never became such an obsession that organised religion took any place in her life. She had within herself a great and driving moral sense that kept her from deviating in any respect from the path she had chosen for herself. She and her sister had both made up their minds early in life, she told me, that they would never marry for fear of passing on the mental taint that was in their heredity. At times she did falter and was perpetually harried by self-doubts and lack of self-confidence. I think her attitude to religion is best summed up in her own words from "Madeleine in Church":

> I do not envy Him His victories,
> His arms are full of broken things.

She did not have any illusions about herself and what people might think of her when they first met her and heard her speak in her rather strident voice and her *méfiant* manner. She describes herself in "Fame":

Sometimes in the over-heated house but not for long,
Smirking and speaking rather loud I see myself among the crowd,
Where no one fits the singer to his song.

The passionate sincerity with which she faced the onslaughts of life can hardly be portrayed more strongly than through lines such as these:

If there were fifty heavens, God could not give us back the child
that went or never came.

She never bolstered herself with subterfuges, she never lurked in stealthy byways stalking the hope of better things in a Better World. She was always conscious, she once admitted, of what seemed to her an earthly presence, a point of actual contact with the earth, "God of final peace in the heart of things". "Nunhead Cemetery" may be taken as her own expression of this belief. She read to the present writer many times a poem (not found among her papers) which described how a Breton shepherd one night left his sheep to lay himself at the foot of a wayside Calvary. Next morning a passer-by found a heap of leaves, all that was left of him. She finished the poem with her characteristic toss of the head, and the admission that for her part such a death, perhaps in a wood, was all she asked; but death came to her in the heart of London surrounded by no trees, no birds, nothing but grey bricks and greyer life.

In order to calm her nerves she always smoked her own hand-made cigarettes in a long cigarette holder. A characteristic attitude was for her to stand beside the fire, one hand on the mantelpiece, one tiny foot (she bought her boots at Pinet's, size 2) of which she was inordinately proud, kicking the fire-bars, shaking her head towards her left shoulder, and swinging a signet ring which she wore on her right-hand little finger round and round in the most fascinating manner by moving her third finger against it. She wore black button boots and thick red worsted stockings, which might only be bought from one special shop.

She would tell stories of her encounter with some war widow or pensioner during her visits on behalf of the War Pensions Committee. I remember the zest with which she once described her arrival in some back street slum, and her knocking at the door, only to be faced by a harridan, with a man's cap worn back to front and a heavy bobbly shawl, towering above her and demanding what she wanted. When told the name of the woman who was sought, the harridan turned and went half-way up the flight of stairs, shrieking in her strident voice, "Tell the lidy upstairs there's a person 'ere who wants to see 'er". Or again of the scene in Somerstown when a whole crowd of dirty little boys were playing War in the street, fighting and pummelling each other, vociferously demanding to be "the prisoner". This unfortunate was placed in a sack and dragged and bumped along the pavement to the cheers of the other boys.

She fully enjoyed London life, every minute of it, however much in her mind she appeared to long for the country. She caught the spirit of London completely in the exquisite little poem "Shade Catchers". This nostalgia for the country and her real, full enjoyment of life in London are again typical of the warring pair within her. So was her complete trust and faith in her friends and her complete distrust and lack of faith in her so-called "business" contacts, although none of them had the slightest desire or inclination to cheat her or twist her in any way. She could not help it. Early in life, so she told me, she had been left a sum of money by an aunt, large or small I do not know, but anyway a lawyer had made away with it and destroyed her faith in Man completely.

Again she showed this singular double personality in that she could seem so gay and so utterly without care that a friend of hers described her thus on a Convent holiday in France, although all the time she was experiencing this great joy in being abroad she was writing letters to

CHARLOTTE MEW AS A GIRL
WITH HER OLD NURSE

*Photo reproduced by courtesy of Sir Sydney Cockerell. The original bears the legend*
*"Artistic Photography at Night by the New Electric Light."*

other friends recounting the misery and discontent she felt away from her normal surroundings. Like many people of character and genius, she was either greatly liked or greatly disliked. She had her detractors but there were many who loved and valued her dearly. She had no need to be despondent in any way as regards her work because from the very first she was successful in finding editors to publish her stories. She contributed for many years to *Temple Bar*, *The Egoist*, *The English Woman* and other journals now defunct stories and poems, particularly the former, which can still hold one's attention but which by the manner in which they are written date them for present day readers. She contributed to the *Yellow Book* one very moving story called "Violets" which dealt with a dying prostitute. Her poems "The Farmer's Bride" (as has been mentioned earlier) and "Saturday Market" appeared in *The Nation* under the editorship of the great H. W. Massingham. Among people who appreciated her work was May Sinclair, now almost forgotten, with whom she had a very complete friendship, until something she heard about Miss Sinclair destroyed it forever. Perhaps one of the great pleasures of her literary success was when she heard that Thomas Hardy admired her poems, in fact so much so that she received an invitation to Max Gate and a pleasant relationship sprang up between them. It was discovered after Hardy's death (which occurred less than two months before her own) that he had copied out her poem "Fin de Fête" on the back of a British Museum Reading Room slip and had it among his personal things in his desk. This copy was given to her by Sir Sydney Cockerell, one of Hardy's executors.

Another sign of her acceptance as a poet was the award to her in December 1923 of a Civil List pension of £75 a year. From the day her poems appeared in book form Charlotte Mew was a success. Most reviews spoke of her originality, of her capacity for putting ideas into the most concise and clear poetic form, and of the rhythm which is so characteristic of her and which was pronounced by every critic to be masterly. She was awarded a Civil List pension on the recommendation of John Masefield, Walter de la Mare and Thomas Hardy; and however much she used to exclaim in private life that she did not care whether or not anyone read her work, the truth is that she was greatly heartened and encouraged by the admiration her poems received from some of her fellow writers, who were most generous in their acceptance of them.

One amusing incident with regard to the publication of her first book, *The Farmer's Bride*, concerned a small firm of printers in Clerkenwell which had printed quite a few books for the Poetry Bookshop and which was sent the manuscript for an estimate. This was duly received and accepted. Some of the galleys had been delivered when one morning the youthful, rosy-cheeked, spectacled son of the printer arrived and very diffidently asked to see Mr. Monro. When they met he became even more diffident than before, and after beating about the bush for some time announced that the compositor, who was a Methodist, had said that he could not set up "Madeleine in Church" as he considered it to be blasphemous. The young man said nothing would move him and as they had only the one compositor, the firm had reluctantly decided it could not undertake the work of printing the book for us. This, as can be imagined, was a sad blow as it upset the whole of our programme, and we were forced to employ a larger printer the other side of the river, whose compositors were not assailed by religious scruples. One of the great difficulties in making the book in the size and format we preferred was the extreme length of the lines, particularly "Madeleine in Church" which Charlotte Mew did not wish to be run over, so that a rather ugly quarto page had to be used. The cover design was specially drawn by C. Lovat Fraser. Charlotte Mew accepted the design, though not with any great enthusiasm.

These two letters written to Harold Monro at the time *The Farmer's Bride* was being seen through the press are of interest in showing her attitude to these matters:

"Many thanks for the proofs in which I have made final corrections which I hope the printer will attend to as they are really important and this is the third time I have tried to get the line in 'The Fête' run on— and if the muddle they have made of the end of 'The Farmer's Bride'— (also corrected in last proofs) remains it will spoil the poem.

"But the two lines run together on page 37 and break in verse on page 38 are also bad mistakes—but when verses intact in last proofs are broken up in these, one feels doubtful, and one only hopes for the best. Can you persuade them to be careful? I think the cover as a cover is first rate but it was so different from what I had in my head that at first sight it gave me a shock. A darkish grey is the colour *I* should like best."

9th February 1916.

"Dear Mr. Monro,

"I think your printer must be a spiritual brother of the editor who refused 'Ken' because 'they believed in the segregation of the feeble minded' and after this one can't expect the advocates of early marriages to buy 'The Farmer's Bride'!

"Thank you for sending the specimen page of which the type etc. seems to me entirely satisfactory. I agree with you that specimen A would make too large a book so that as something must be sacrificed to the abnormal lines of 'Madeleine' (which I am sure should not turn over) it looks as if it must be the margin. I am afraid the whole poem is going to be tiresome—is the spacing etc. left altogether to the printer——?"

It is interesting to have this record of the close attention Charlotte Mew paid to the appearance of her poems on a page. It was quite impossible to make her understand that certain exigencies of space prevented the printer, however much he might wish to carry out her directions, from having the lines the full width of the page. These letters also show, what she herself always declared to be the case, that she hadn't the faintest idea how to punctuate. She gave the present writer *carte blanche* to correct the punctuation of her poems as she might think fit.

I quote two further extracts from letters to her friends about her work. The first is written from Boulogne in 1911: "It makes all the difference to me to be in the right place. And I should never have done 'Fête' if I hadn't been here last year. One realises the place much more alone I think—it is all there is—you don't feel it through another mind which mixes up things—I wonder if Art—as they say, is a rather inhuman thing? Anyhow one can't choose the working of it and here I feel even the sea for seeing things is distracting and if I do anything shall have to get away from it to some quiet place".

The second is written from 9, Gordon Street, July 24, 1913, to Mrs. Hill: "I have to and do most gratefully thank you for a very fine criticism of the verse (returned yesterday) or whatever you like to call it—so far I have only had a general 'appreciation' and your detailed one is more helpful and valuable, nor if I may say so, without impertinence do the experts or literary people seem to get closely to it or judge it as acutely. I am glad you like 'Fame' which I personally prefer to anything I have done though I don't know why and curiously enough 'The

Quiet House' which you say you see objectively is perhaps the most subjective to me, of the lot. I wanted in 'Ken' to do what you say I have done, i.e. obscured the tragic side by a tenderness of treatment—and for 'Nunhead'—the last verse which you find superfluous is to me the most inevitable—(and was written first)—being a lapse from the sanity and self-control of what precedes it—the mind—and senses can stand no more—and that is to express their failure and exhaustion—I shouldn't have bothered you with all this if you hadn't in a sense asked for it. I've things now in my head rather unmanageable and possibly too big to pull off as in this form I am really a beginner. Mrs. Dawson Scott asked me to go down last Saturday and recite the poem to some literary friends and in my brightest way I replied that she had mistaken me for Little Titch or Margaret Cooper at the piano and impolitely declined; but got a note on Saturday to say she was ill and Damn she would not write to me again! So I went down to inquire and found her up again and was made to stay to dinner and talked a lot of literary shop and commenting on some remark of hers I said it was one of the things you didn't say. 'But it's true' she protested, to which even more light-heartedly I replied, 'Many things are true which only the commonest minds observe'. However, the goose that lays their golden eggs does not really count and she asked me down to Cornwall where they have a cottage for the summer, but I can't see my way to go."

Looking back on Charlotte Mew's published work it is difficult to understand how it was that so gifted a woman should have produced so little in the sixty years given to her. Many writers give up in despair at failing to place their work, but such was not her case. From the very first she found a ready market for her stories—the poems were a later development of her talent. She wrote a one-act play in Cornish dialect, *The China Bowl,* which shows her sense of drama at its best; Violet Vanbrugh intended producing it, but circumstances prevented her from doing so, and to Charlotte's intense disappointment no more was heard of it. I think from what she said this was one of the great disappointments of her life, and, characteristically, being disappointed she threw the MS. into a drawer and left it there. She herself attributed her small output to the difficulties of domestic life, doing the housekeeping and looking after "Ma", and the constant interruptions when she sat at her desk—Jane, the factotum who was with her for years, knocking on the door to ask if

# Sea Love

=

Tide be runnin' the great world over:
'Twas only last June month I mind that we
~~Dear the~~ the toss o' the call on the weast of
Was thinkin' in'
                                          the river

So everlasting as the sea

Heer's the same little fishes that splutter & swim;
in' Yes the moon's oad gloin' an the grey, wet, sand;
And him no more to me nor me to him
Than the wind goin' over my hand.

≥

Charlotte Mew.

A POEM IN MANUSCRIPT

*Sea Love* (see p. 44): the author's own corrected copy, reproduced about three-quarters the size of the original.

she should "finish up" the rice pudding for her dinner? and should she run out for some kippers? or would Miss Lottie mind going herself?

I think myself that as she grew older she no longer had the power of concentration required to sit at a desk for hours at a time, that she lost interest in story writing which had been her main work till about 1916, after which she wrote no more prose at all and very little verse. The sustained prose work dwindled from the long stories printed in *Temple Bar* in the 'nineties to short studies and occasional essays in the early 1900s, and then to odd poems, and slowly work came to a standstill. Also I think she was afflicted with a certain dilettante outlook, perhaps the result of her education, which was the limited one of the 1870s and 80s, and also was partly influenced by her mother's attitude to a daughter with a career. No one in the family except Anne took her work seriously. She was almost fifty when her first book *The Farmer's Bride* (1916) appeared, and although she was greatly encouraged by its reception she wasn't capable by then of writing much more. Few of the poems which were published posthumously in *The Rambling Sailor* (1929) were written after 1916. She always spoke of stacks of MSS. salted away in trunks, but after her death very little was found. Perhaps there was some truth in the remark she once made casually to me one afternoon at tea in Gordon Street. She was sitting making spills, which she used to light her endless cigarettes, and which were also made for the parrot to chew and amuse himself with. Seeing some writing on some of these, I asked if she used up old letters that way, and she replied—"I'm burning up my work. I don't know what else to do with it". Anne and I often wondered together whether she might be really destroying some original work, or whether it was just intended to whip us up. Who knows?

Only 500 copies of *The Farmer's Bride* were printed, price one shilling, and they took years to sell out; and yet out of that tiny edition came a great reputation. We published what was to us this big edition— many of the books that came from the Poetry Bookshop had only 250 copies for their first edition—because we felt that in Charlotte Mew there was a poet whose work would justify our faith. Time has shown that we were right.

# EARLY POEMS

## *At the Convent Gate*

"WHY do you shrink away, and start and stare?
    Life frowns to see you leaning at death's gate—
    Not back, but on. Ah! sweet, it is too late:
You cannot cast these kisses from your hair.
Will God's cold breath blow kindly anywhere
      Upon such burning gold? Oh! lips worn white
      With waiting! Love will blossom in a night
And you shall wake to find the roses there!"

"Oh hush! He seems to stir, He lifts His Head.
He smiles. Look where He hangs against the sky.
He never smiled nor stirred, that God of pain
With tired eyes and limbs above my bed—
But loose me, this is death, I will not die—
Not while He smiles. Oh! Christ, Thine own again!"

## *Requiescat*

YOUR birds that call from tree to tree
    Just overhead, and whirl and dart,
Your breeze fresh-blowing from the sea,
    And your sea singing on, Sweetheart.

Your salt scent on the thin sharp air
  Of this grey dawn's first drowsy hours,
While on the grass shines everywhere
  The yellow starlight of your flowers.

At the road's end your strip of blue
  Beyond that line of naked trees—
Strange that we should remember you
  As if you would remember these!

As if your spirit, swaying yet
  To the old passions, were not free
Of Spring's wild magic, and the fret
  Of the wilder wooing of the sea!

What threat of old imaginings,
  Half-haunted joy, enchanted pain,
Or dread of unfamiliar things
  Should ever trouble you again?

Yet you would wake and want, you said,
  The little whirr of wings, the clear
Gay notes, the wind, the golden bed
  Of the daffodil: and they are here!

Just overhead, they whirl and dart
  Your birds that call from tree to tree,
Your sea is singing on—Sweetheart,
  Your breeze is blowing from the sea.

Beyond the line of naked trees
  At the road's end, your stretch of blue—
Strange if you should remember these
  As we, ah! God! remember you!

## *The Little Portress*

(ST. GILDA DE RHUYS)

THE stillness of the sunshine lies
   Upon her spirit: silence seems
   To look out from its place of dreams
When suddenly she lifts her eyes
   To waken, for a little space,
   The smile asleep upon her face.

A thousand years of sun and shower,
   The melting of unnumbered snows
   Go to the making of the rose
Which blushes out its little hour.
   So old is Beauty: in its heart
   The ages seem to meet and part.

Like Beauty's self, she holds a clear
   Deep memory of hidden things—
   The music of forgotten springs—
So far she travels back, so near
   She seems to stand to patient truth,
   As old as Age, as young as Youth.

That is her window, by the gate.
   Now and again her figure flits
   Across the wall. Long hours she sits
Within: on all who come to wait.
   Her Saviour too is hanging there
   A foot or so above her chair.

"Sœur Marie de l'enfant Jésus,"
   You wrote it in my little book—
   Your shadow-name. Your shadow-look
Is dimmer and diviner too,
   But not to keep: it slips so far
   Beyond us to that golden bar

Where angels, watching from their stair,
   Half-envy you your tranquil days
   Of prayer as exquisite as praise,—
Grey twilights softer than their glare

Of glory: all sweet human things
Which vanish with the whirr of wings.

Yet will you, when you wing your way
    To whiter worlds, more whitely shine
    Or shed a radiance more divine
Than here you shed from day to day—
    High in His heaven a quiet star,
    Be nearer God than now you are?

## Afternoon Tea

PLEASE you, excuse me, good five-o'clock people,
    I've lost my last hatful of words,
And my heart's in the wood up above the church steeple,
    I'd rather have tea with the birds.

Gay Kate's stolen kisses, poor Barnaby's scars,
    John's losses and Mary's gains,
Oh! what do they matter, my dears, to the stars
    Or the glow-worms in the lanes!

I'd rather lie under the tall elm-trees,
    With old rooks talking loud overhead,
To watch a red squirrel run over my knees,
    Very still on my brackeny bed.

And wonder what feathers the wrens will be taking
    For lining their nests next Spring;
Or why the tossed shadow of boughs in a great wind shaking
    Is such a lovely thing.

## *She was a Sinner*

Love was my flower, and before He came—
        "Master, there was a garden where it grew
Rank, with the colour of a crimson flame,
        Thy flower too, but knowing not its name
Nor yet that it was Thine, I did not spare
But tore and trampled it and stained my hair,
My hands, my lips, with the red petals; see,
        Drenched with the blood of Thy poor murdered flower
I stood, when suddenly the hour
                Struck for me,
And straight I came and wound about Thy Feet
                The strands of shame
Twined with those broken buds: till lo, more sweet,
                More red, yet still the same,
Bright burning blossoms sprang around Thy brow
Beneath the thorns (I saw, I know not how,
The crown which Thou wast afterward to wear
                On that immortal Tree)
And I went out and found my garden very bare,
But swept and watered it, then followed Thee.

There was another garden where to seek
Thee, first, I came in those grey hours
Of the Great Dawn, and knew Thee not till Thou didst speak
My name, that 'Mary' like a flash of light
Shot from Thy lips. Thou wast 'the gardener' too,
                And then I knew
That evermore our flowers,
Thine, Lord, and mine, shall be a burning white."

## Song

OH! Sorrow, Sorrow, scarce I knew
    Your name when, shaking down the may
In sport, a little child, I grew
    Afraid to find you at my play.
I heard it ere I looked at you;
    You sang it softly as you came
Bringing your little boughs of yew
    To fling across my gayest game.

Oh! Sorrow, Sorrow, was I fair
    That when I decked me for a bride,
You met me stepping down the stair
    And led me from my lover's side?
Was I so dear you could not spare
    The maid to love, the child to play,
But coming always unaware,
    Must bid and beckon me away?

Oh! Sorrow, Sorrow, is my bed
    So wide and warm that you must lie
Upon it; toss your weary head
    And stir my slumber with your sigh?
I left my love at your behest,
    I waved your little boughs of yew,
But, Sorrow, Sorrow, let me rest,
    For oh! I cannot sleep with you!

# POEMS FROM FRANCE

### The Narrow Door

THE narrow door, the narrow door
   On the three steps of which the café children play
   Mostly at shop with pebbles from the shore,
   It is always shut this narrow door
But open for a little while to-day.

And round it, each with pebbles in his hand,
A silenced crowd the café children stand
To see the long box jerking down the bend
Of twisted stair; then set on end,
Quite filling up the narrow door
Till it comes out and does not go in any more.

   Along the quay you see it wind,
The slow black line. Someone pulls up the blind
Of the small window just above the narrow door—
   "*Tiens! que veux-tu acheter?*" Renée cries,
   "*Mais, pour quat' sous, des oignons,*" Jean replies,
And one pays down with pebbles from the shore.

## The Fête

To-night again the moon's white mat
    Stretches across the dormitory floor
While outside, like an evil cat
    The *pion* prowls down the dark corridor,
    Planning, I know, to pounce on me, in spite
For getting leave to sleep in town last night.
But it was none of us who made that noise,
    Only the old brown owl that hoots and flies
Out of the ivy—he will say it was us boys—
    *Seigneur mon Dieu:* the *sacré* soul of spies!
    He would like to catch each dream that lies
        Hidden behind our sleepy eyes:
Their dream? But mine—it is the moon and the wood that sees;
All my long life how I shall hate the trees!

In the *Place d'Armes* the dusty planes, all Summer through,
Dozed with the market women in the sun and scarcely stirred
    To see the quiet things that crossed the Square—,
A tiny funeral, the flying shadow of a bird,
    The hump-backed barber Célestin Lemaire,
    Old Madame Michel in her three-wheeled chair,
        And filing past to Vespers, two and two,
        The *demoiselles* of the *pensionnat*
Towed like a ship through the harbour bar,
    Safe into port, where *le petit Jésus*
Perhaps makes nothing of the look they shot at you:
    *Si, c'est défendu, mais que voulez-vous?*
It was the sun. The sunshine weaves
A pattern on dull stones: the sunshine leaves
    The portraiture of dreams upon the eyes
        Before it dies:
    All Summer through
The dust hung white upon the drowsy planes
Till suddenly they woke with the Autumn rains.

    It is not only the little boys
    Who have hardly got away from toys,
But I, who am seventeen next year,
Some nights, in bed, have grown cold to hear

That lonely passion of the rain
Which makes you think of being dead,
And of somewhere living to lay your head
  As if you were a child again,
Crying for one thing, known and near
Your empty heart, to still the hunger and the fear
  That pelts and beats with it against the pane.


  But I remember smiling too
At all the sun's soft tricks and those Autumn dreads
  In winter time, when the grey light broke slowly through
The frosted window-lace to drag us shivering from our beds.
  And when at dusk the singing wind swung down
Straight from the stars to the dark country roads
          Beyond the twinkling town,
  Striking the leafless poplar boughs as he went by,
Like some poor, stray dog by the wayside lying dead,
We left behind us the old world of dread,
I and the wind as we strode whistling on under the Winter sky.


And then in Spring for three days came the Fair
  Just as the planes were starting into bud
Above the caravans: you saw the dancing bear
  Pass on his chain; and heard the jingle and the thud.
      Only four days ago
      They let you out of this dull show
To slither down the *montagne russe* and chaff the man *à la tête de veau*
      Hit, slick, the bull's eye at the *tir*,
Spin round and round till your head went queer
On the *porcs-roulants. Oh! là là! fête!*
*Va pour du vin, et le tête-a-tête*
With the girl who sugars the *gaufres! Pauvrette*,
  How thin she was! but she smiled, you bet,


  As she took your tip—"One does not forget
The good days, Monsieur". Said with a grace,
But *sacrebleu:* what a ghost of a face!
  And no fun too for the *demoiselles*
Of the *pensionnat*, who were hurried past,
  With their "*Oh, que c'est beau—Ah, qu'elle est belle!*"
A lap-dog's life from first to last!

The good nights are not made for sleep, nor the good days for dreaming in,
    And at the end in the big Circus tent we sat and shook and stewed like sin!


    Some children there had got—but where?
Sent from the south, perhaps—a red bouquet
    Of roses, sweetening the fetid air
With scent from gardens by some far away blue bay.
    They threw one at the dancing bear;
The white clown caught it. From St. Rémy's tower
    The deep, slow bell tolled out the hour;
The black clown, with his dirty grin
    Lay, sprawling in the dust, as She rode in.


She stood on a white horse—and suddenly you saw the bend
    Of a far-off road at dawn, with knights riding by,
A field of spears—and then the gallant day
Go out in storm, with ragged clouds low down, sullen and grey
    Against red heavens: wild and awful, such a sky
    As witnesses against you at the end
Of a great battle; bugles blowing, blood and dust—
The old *Morte d'Arthur*, fight you must—.
    It died in anger. But it was not death
    That had you by the throat, stopping your breath.
She looked like Victory. She rode my way.


She laughed at the black clown and then she flew
        A bird above us, on the wing
Of her white arms; and you saw through
A rent in the old tent, a patch of sky
With one dim star. She flew, but not so high—
        And then she did not fly;
She stood in the bright moonlight at the door
Of a strange room, she threw her slippers on the floor—
          Again, again
        You heard the patter of the rain,
        The starving rain—it was this Thing,
Summer was this, the gold mist in your eyes;—
          Oh God! it dies,
          But after death—,
    To-night the splendour and the sting
    Blows back and catches at your breath,

The smell of beasts, the smell of dust, the scent of all the roses in the world,
     the sea, the Spring,
The beat of drums, the pad of hoofs, music, the dream, the dream, the
     Enchanted Thing!

  At first you scarcely saw her face,
  You knew the maddening feet were there,
What called was that half-hidden, white unrest
To which now and then she pressed
  Her finger-tips; but as she slackened pace
And turned and looked at you it grew quite bare:
     There was not anything you did not dare:—
Like trumpeters the hours passed until the last day of the Fair.

  In the *Place d'Armes* all afternoon
  The building birds had sung "Soon, soon",
The shuttered streets slept sound that night,
     It was full moon:
The path into the wood was almost white,
The trees were very still and seemed to stare:
  Not far before your soul the Dream flits on,
  But when you touch it, it is gone
And quite alone your soul stands there.

Mother of Christ, no one has seen your eyes: how can men pray
     Even unto you?
There were only wolves' eyes in the wood—
     My Mother is a woman too:
Nothing is true that is not good,
With that quick smile of hers, I have heard her say;—
I wish I had gone back home to-day;
  I should have watched the light that so gently dies
  From our high window, in the Paris skies,
     The long, straight chain
  Of lamps hung out along the Seine:
I would have turned to her and let the rain
Beat on her breast as it does against the pane;—
  Nothing will be the same again;—
There is something strange in my little Mother's eyes,
There is something new in the old heavenly air of Spring—
The smell of beasts, the smell of dust—*The Enchanted Thing!*

All my life long I shall see moonlight on the fern
   And the black trunks of trees. Only the hair
Of any woman can belong to God.
The stalks are cruelly broken where we trod,
       There had been violets there,
       I shall not care
As I used to do when I see the bracken burn.

## *Pécheresse*

D<small>OWN</small> the long quay the slow boats glide,
   While here and there a house looms white
Against the gloom of the waterside,
   And some high window throws a light
   As they sail out into the night.

At dawn they will bring in again
   To women knitting on the quay
Who wait for him, their man of men;
   I stand with them, and watch the sea
   Which may have taken mine from me.

Just so the long days come and go.
   The nights, ma Doué! the nights are cold!
Our Lady's heart is as frozen snow,
   Since this one sin I have not told;
   And I shall die or perhaps grow old

Before he comes. The foreign ships
   Bring many a one of face and name
As strange as his, to buy your lips,
   A gold piece for a scarlet shame
   Like mine. But mine was not the same.

One night was ours, one short grey day
   Of sudden sin, unshrived, untold.
He found me, and I lost the way

To Paradise for him. I sold
My soul for love and not for gold.

He bought my soul, but even so,
　My face is all that he has seen,
His is the only face I know,
And in the dark church, like a screen,
　It shuts God out; it comes between.

While in some narrow foreign street
　Or loitering on the crowded quay,
Who knows what others he may meet
　To turn his eyes away from me?
　Many are fair to such as he!

There is but one for such as I
　To love, to hate, to hunger for;
I shall, perhaps, grow old and die,
With one short day to spend and store,
　One night, in all my life, no more.

Just so the long days come and go,
　Yet this one sin I will not tell
Though Mary's heart is as frozen snow
And all nights are cold for one warmed too well.
　But, oh! ma Doué! *the nights of Hell!*

## *Jour des Morts*

### (CIMETIÈRE MONTPARNASSE)

SWEETHEART, is this the last of all our posies
　And little festivals, my flowers are they
But white and wistful ghosts of gayer roses
　Shut with you in this grim garden? Not to-day,
Ah! no! come out with me before the grey gate closes
　It is your fête and here is your bouquet!

33

## *Madeleine in Church*

Hᴇʀᴇ, in the darkness, where this plaster saint
    Stands nearer than God stands to our distress,
And one small candle shines, but not so faint
    As the far lights of everlastingness,
I'd rather kneel than over there, in open day
      Where Christ is hanging, rather pray
        To something more like my own clay,
           Not too divine;
      For, once, perhaps my little saint
      Before he got his niche and crown,
Had one short stroll about the town;
It brings him closer, just that taint—
      And anyone can wash the paint
Off our poor faces, his and mine!

Is that why I see Monty now? equal to any saint, poor boy, as good as gold,
But still, with just the proper trace
Of earthliness on his shining wedding face;
And then gone suddenly blank and old
The hateful day of the divorce:
Stuart got his, hands down, of course
Crowing like twenty cocks and grinning like a horse:
But Monty took it hard. All said and done I liked him best,—
He was the first, he stands out clearer than the rest.
          It seems too funny all we other rips
      Should have immortal souls; Monty and Redge quite damnably
      Keep theirs afloat while we go down like scuttled ships.—
          It's funny too, how easily we sink,
            One might put up a monument, I think
            To half the world and cut across it "Lost at Sea!"
I should drown Jim, poor little sparrow, if I netted him to-night—
          No, it's no use this penny light—
          Or my poor saint with his tin-pot crown—
          The trees of Calvary are where they were,
            When we are sure that we can spare
            The tallest, let us go and strike it down
And leave the other two still standing there.
              I, too, would ask Him to remember me
If there were any Paradise beyond this earth that I could see.

Oh! quiet Christ who never knew
The poisonous fangs that bite us through
And make us do the things we do,
See how we suffer and fight and die,
How helpless and how low we lie,
God holds You, and You hang so high,
Though no one looking long at You,
Can think You do not suffer too,
But, up there, from your still, star-lighted tree
What can You know, what can You really see
Of this dark ditch, the soul of me!


We are what we are: when I was half a child I could not sit
Watching black shadows on green lawns and red carnations burning in the sun,
Without paying so heavily for it
That joy and pain, like any mother and her unborn child were almost one.
I could hardly bear
The dreams upon the eyes of white geraniums in the dusk,
The thick, close voice of musk,
The jessamine music on the thin night air,
Or, sometimes, my own hands about me anywhere—
The sight of my own face (for it was lovely then) even the scent of my own hair,
Oh! there was nothing, nothing that did not sweep to the high seat
Of laughing gods, and then blow down and beat
My soul into the highway dust, as hoofs do the dropped roses of the street.
I think my body was my soul,
And when we are made thus
Who shall control
Our hands, our eyes, the wandering passion of our feet,
Who shall teach us
To thrust the world out of our heart: to say, till perhaps in death,
When the race is run,
And it is forced from us with our last breath
"Thy will be done"?
If it is Your will that we should be content with the tame, bloodless things.
As pale as angels smirking by, with folded wings—
Oh! I know Virtue, and the peace it brings!
The temperate, well-worn smile
The one man gives you, when you are evermore his own:
And afterwards the child's, for a little while,
With its unknowing and all-seeing eyes

So soon to change, and make you feel how quick
The clock goes round. If one had learned the trick—
      (How does one though?) quite early on,
Of long green pastures under placid skies,
One might be walking now with patient truth.
What did we ever care for it, who have asked for youth,
   When, oh! my God! this is going or has gone?


  There is a portrait of my mother, at nineteen,
With the black spaniel, standing by the garden seat,
The dainty head held high against the painted green
And throwing out the youngest smile, shy, but half haughty and half sweet.
Her picture then: but simply Youth, or simply Spring
  To me to-day: a radiance on the wall,
  So exquisite, so heart-breaking a thing
Beside the mask that I remember, shrunk and small,
   Sapless and lined like a dead leaf,
All that was left of oh! the loveliest face, by time and grief!


And in the glass, last night, I saw a ghost behind my chair—
Yet why remember it, when one can still go moderately gay—?
 Or could—with any one of the old crew,
   But oh! these boys! the solemn way
 They take you and the things they say—
 This "I have only as long as you"
When you remind them you are not precisely twenty-two—
  Although at heart perhaps—God! if it were
   Only the face, only the hair!
  If Jim had written to me as he did to-day
  A year ago—and now it leaves me cold—
   I know what this means, old, old, *old:*
   *Et avec ça—mais on a vécu, tout se paie.*


That is not always true: there was my Mother (well at least the dead are free!)
  Yoked to the man that Father was; yoked to the woman I am, Monty too,
  The little portress at the Convent School, stewing in hell so patiently;
The poor, fair boy who shot himself at Aix. And what of me—and what of me?
  But I, I paid for what I had, and they for nothing. No, one cannot see
   How it shall be made up to them in some serene eternity.
If there were fifty heavens God could not give us back the child who went or never
  came;

Here, on our little patch of this great earth, the sun of any darkened day,
Not one of all the starry buds hung on the hawthorn trees of last year's May,
No shadow from the sloping fields of yesterday;
For every hour they slant across the hedge a different way,
The shadows are never the same.


"Find rest in Him!" One knows the parsons' tags—
Back to the fold, across the evening fields, like any flock of baa-ing sheep:
Yes, it may be, when He has shorn, led us to slaughter, torn the bleating soul in us
to rags,
For so He giveth His belovèd sleep.
Oh! He will take us stripped and done,
Driven into His heart. So we are won:
Then safe, safe are we? in the shelter of His everlasting wings—
I do not envy Him his victories, His arms are full of broken things.


But I shall not be in them. Let Him take
The finer ones, the easier to break.
And they are not gone, yet, for me, the lights, the colours, the perfumes,
Though now they speak rather in sumptuous rooms,
In silks and in gem-like wines;
Here, even, in this corner where my little candle shines
And overhead the lancet-window glows
With golds and crimsons you could almost drink
To know how jewels taste, just as I used to think
There was the scent in every red and yellow rose
Of all the sunsets. But this place is grey,
And much too quiet. No one here,
Why, this is awful, this is fear!
Nothing to see, no face,
Nothing to hear except your heart beating in space
As if the world was ended. Dead at last!
Dead soul, dead body, tied together fast.
These to go on with and alone, to the slow end:
No one to sit with, really, or to speak to, friend to friend:
Out of the long procession, black or white or red
Not one left now to say "Still I am here, then see you, dear, lay here your head".
Only the doll's house looking on the Park
To-night, all nights, I know, when the man puts the lights out, very dark.
With, upstairs, in the blue and gold box of a room, just the maids' footsteps overhead,
Then utter silence and the empty world—the room—the bed—

The corpse! No, not quite dead, while this cries out in me,
But nearly: very soon to be
A handful of forgotten dust—
There must be someone. Christ! there must,
Tell me there *will* be someone. Who?
If there were no one else, could it be You?

How old was Mary out of whom you cast
So many devils? Was she young or perhaps for years
She had sat staring, with dry eyes, at this and that man going past
Till suddenly she saw You on the steps of Simeon's house
And stood and looked at You through tears.
I think she must have known by those
The thing, for what it was that had come to her
For some of us there is a passion, I suppose,
So far from earthly cares and earthly fears
That in its stillness you can hardly stir
Or in its nearness, lift your hand,
So great that you have simply got to stand
Looking at it through tears, through tears.
Then straight from these there broke the kiss,
I think You must have known by this
The thing, for what it was, that had come to You:
She did not love You like the rest,
It was in her own way, but at the worst, the best,
She gave You something altogether new.
And through it all, from her, no word,
She scarcely saw You, scarcely heard:
Surely You knew when she so touched You with her hair,
Or by the wet cheek lying there,
And while her perfume clung to You from head to feet all through the day
That You can change the things for which we care,
But even You, unless You kill us, not the way.

This, then was peace for her, but passion too.
I wonder was it like a kiss that once I knew,
The only one that I would care to take
Into the grave with me, to which, if there were afterwards, to wake.
Almost as happy as the carven dead
In some dim chancel lying head by head
We slept with it, but face to face, the whole night through—

One breath, one throbbing quietness, as if the thing behind our lips was endless life,
    Lost, as I woke, to hear in the strange earthly dawn, his "Are you there?"
            And lie still, listening to the wind outside, among the firs.


    So Mary chose the dream of Him for what was left to her of night and day,
It is the only truth: it is the dream in us that neither life nor death nor any other
            thing can take away:
    But if she had not touched Him in the doorway of the dream could she have
            cared so much?
    She was a sinner, we are what we are: the spirit afterwards, but first the touch.


And He has never shared with me my haunted house beneath the trees
Of Eden and Calvary, with its ghosts that have not any eyes for tears,
And the happier guests who would not see, or if they did, remember these,
            Though they lived there a thousand years.
        Outside, too gravely looking at me, He seems to stand,
          And looking at Him, if my forgotten spirit came
            Unwillingly back, what could it claim
             Of those calm eyes, that quiet speech,
          Breaking like a slow tide upon the beach,
            The scarred, not quite human hand?—
      Unwillingly back to the burden of old imaginings
      When it has learned so long not to think, not to be,
Again, again it would speak as it has spoken to me of things
           That I shall not see!


    I cannot bear to look at this divinely bent and gracious head:
      When I was small I never quite believed that He was dead:
      And at the Convent school I used to lie awake in bed
Thinking about His hands. It did not matter what they said,
He was alive to me, so hurt, so hurt! And most of all in Holy Week
      When there was no one else to see
      I used to think it would not hurt me too, so terribly,
        If He had ever seemed to notice me
        Or if, for once, He would only speak.

## Le Sacré-Cœur

*(Montmartre)*

I<small>T</small> is dark up here on the heights,
    Between the dome and the stars it is quiet too,
While down there under the crowded lights
    Flares the importunate face of you,
Dear Paris of the hot white hands, the scarlet lips, the scented hair,
    *Une jolie fille à vendre, très cher;*
      A thing of gaiety, a thing of sorrow,
      Bought to-night, possessed, and tossed
      Back to the mart again to-morrow,
        Worth and over, what you cost;
While half your charm is that you are,
Withal, like some unpurchaseable star,
    So old, so young and infinite and lost.

It is dark on the dome-capped hill,
    Serenely dark, divinely still,
Yet here is the Man who bought you first
    Dying of his immortal smart,
Your Lover, the King with the broken heart,
    Who while you, feasting, drink your fill,
      Pass round the cup
      Not looking up,
Calls down to you, "I thirst".

"A King with a broken heart! *Mon Dieu!*
    One breaks so many, *cela peut se croire,*
To remember all *c'est la mer à boire,*
    And the first, *mais comme c'est vieux.*
Perhaps there is still some keepsake—or
    One has possibly sold it for a song:
*On ne peut pas toujours pleurer les morts,*
    And this One—He has been dead so long!"

## *Monsieur qui Passe*

QUAI VOLTAIRE

A PURPLE blot against the dead white door
In my friend's rooms, bathed in their vile pink light,
I had not noticed her before
She snatched my eyes and threw them back at me:
She did not speak till we came out into the night,
Paused at this bench beside the kiosk on the quay.

God knows precisely what she said—
I left to her the twisted skein,
Though here and there I caught a thread,—
Something, at first, about "the lamps along the Seine,
And Paris, with that witching card of Spring
Kept up her sleeve,—why you could see
The trick done on these freezing winter nights!
While half the kisses of the Quay—
Youth, hope,—the whole enchanted string
Of dreams hung on the Seine's long line of lights".

Then suddenly she stripped, the very skin
Came off her soul,—a mere girl clings
Longer to some last rag, however thin,
When she has shown you—well—all sorts of things:
"If it were daylight—oh! one keeps one's head—
But fourteen years!—No one has ever guessed—
The whole thing starts when one gets to bed—
Death?—If the dead would tell us they had rest!
But your eyes held it as I stood there by the door—
One speaks to Christ—one tries to catch His garment's hem—
One hardly says as much to Him—no more:
It was not you, it was your eyes—I spoke to them".

She stopped like a shot bird that flutters still,
And drops, and tries to run again, and swerves.
The tale should end in some walled house upon a hill.
My eyes, at least, won't play such havoc there,—
Or hers—— But she had hair!—blood dipped in gold;
And here she left me throwing back the first odd stare.
Some sort of beauty once, but turning yellow, getting old.
Pouah! These women and their nerves!
God! but the night *is* cold!

# POEMS FROM THE
# ENGLISH COUNTRYSIDE

### The Farmer's Bride

THREE Summers since I chose a maid,
  Too young maybe—but more's to do
At harvest-time than bide and woo.
   When us was wed she turned afraid
Of love and me and all things human;
Like the shut of a winter's day
Her smile went out, and 'twadn't a woman—
   More like a little frightened fay.
    One night, in the Fall, she runned away.

"Out 'mong the sheep, her be," they said,
'Should properly have been abed;
But sure enough she wadn't there
Lying awake with her wide brown stare.
So over seven-acre field and up-along across the down
  We chased her, flying like a hare
Before our lanterns. To Church-Town
   All in a shiver and a scare
We caught her, fetched her home at last
   And turned the key upon her, fast.

She does the work about the house
As well as most, but like a mouse:
   Happy enough to chat and play
   With birds and rabbits and such as they,
   So long as men-folk keep away.

"Not near, not near!" her eyes beseech
When one of us comes within reach.
    The women say that beasts in stall
    Look round like children at her call.
    I've hardly heard her speak at all.

Shy as a leveret, swift as he,
Straight and slight as a young larch tree,
Sweet as the first wild violets, she,
To her wild self. But what to me?

The short days shorten and the oaks are brown,
    The blue smoke rises to the low grey sky,
One leaf in the still air falls slowly down,
    A magpie's spotted feathers lie
On the black earth spread white with rime,
The berries redden up to Christmas-time.
    What's Christmas-time without there be
    Some other in the house than we!

    She sleeps up in the attic there
    Alone, poor maid. 'Tis but a stair
Betwixt us. Oh! my God! the down,
The soft young down of her, the brown,
The brown of her—her eyes, her hair, her hair!


*Arracombe Wood*

SOME said, because he wud'n spaik
    Any words to women but Yes and No,
Nor put out his hand for Parson to shake
    He mun be bird-witted. But I do go
    By the lie of the barley that he did sow,
And I wish no better thing than to hold a rake
    Like Dave, in his time, or to see him mow.

    Put up in churchyard a month ago,
"A bitter old soul", they said, but it wadn't so.
His heart were in Arracombe Wood where he'd used to go

To sit and talk wi' his shadder till sun went low,
Though what it was all about us'll never know.
    And there baint no mem'ry in the place
    Of th' old man's footmark, nor his face;
    Arracombe Wood do think more of a crow—
'Will be violets there in the Spring: in Summer time the spider's lace;
    And come the Fall, the whizzle and race
Of the dry, dead leaves when the wind gies chase;
    And on the Eve of Christmas, fallin' snow.


## Sea Love

Tide be runnin' the great world over:
    'Twas only last June month I mind that we
Was thinkin' the toss and the call in the breast of the lover
    So everlastin' as the sea.

Heer's the same little fishes that sputter and swim,
    Wi' the moon's old glim on the grey, wet sand;
An' him no more to me nor me to him
    Than the wind goin' over my hand.


## In the Fields

Lord, when I look at lovely things which pass,
    Under old trees the shadows of young leaves
Dancing to please the wind along the grass,
    Or the gold stillness of the August sun on the August sheaves;
Can I believe there is a heavenlier world than this?
    And if there is
Will the strange heart of any everlasting thing
    Bring me these dreams that take my breath away?
They come at evening with the home-flying rooks and the scent of hay,
    Over the fields. They come in Spring.

## Old Shepherd's Prayer

Up to the bed by the window, where I be lyin',
Comes bells and bleat of the flock wi' they two children's clack.
Over, from under the eaves there's the starlings flyin',
And down in yard, fit to burst his chain, yapping out at Sue I do hear young Mac.

Turning around like a falled-over sack
I can see team ploughin' in Whithy-bush field and meal carts startin' up road to
    Church-Town;
Saturday arternoon the men goin' back
And the women from market, trapin' home over the down.

Heavenly Master, I wud like to wake to they same green places
Where I be know'd for breakin' dogs and follerin' sheep.
And if I may not walk in th' old ways and look on th' old faces
I wud sooner sleep.

# PERSONAL POEMS

## *Fame*

SOMETIMES in the over-heated house, but not for long,
    Smirking and speaking rather loud,
      I see myself among the crowd,
Where no one fits the singer to his song,
Or sifts the unpainted from the painted faces
Of the people who are always on my stair;
They were not with me when I walked in heavenly places;
      But could I spare
In the blind Earth's great silences and spaces,
    The din, the scuffle, the long stare
    If I went back and it was not there?
Back to the old known things that are the new,
The folded glory of the gorse, the sweet-briar air,
To the larks that cannot praise us, knowing nothing of what we do,
    And the divine, wise trees that do not care.
Yet, to leave Fame, still with such eyes and that bright hair!
God! If I might! And before I go hence
      Take in her stead
      To our tossed bed
One little dream, no matter how small, how wild.
Just now, I think I found it in a field, under a fence—
A frail, dead, new-born lamb, ghostly and pitiful and white,
      A blot upon the night,
The moon's dropped child!

## *The Pedlar*

L END me, a little while, the key
    That locks your heavy heart, and I'll give you back—
Rarer than books and ribbons and beads bright to see,
    This little Key of Dreams out of my pack.

The road, the road, beyond men's bolted doors,
    There shall I walk and you go free of me,
For yours lies North across the moors,
    And mine South. To what sea?

How if we stopped and let our solemn selves go by,
    While my gay ghost caught and kissed yours, as ghosts don't do,
And by the wayside this forgotten you and I
    Sat, and were twenty-two?

Give me the key that locks your tired eyes,
    And I will lend you this one from my pack,
Brighter than coloured beads and painted books that make men wise:
    Take it. No, give it back!

## *À Quoi Bon Dire*

S EVENTEEN years ago you said
    Something that sounded like Good-bye;
        And everybody thinks that you are dead,
            But I.

    So I, as I grow stiff and cold
    To this and that say Good-bye too;
        And everybody sees that I am old
            But you.

    And one fine morning in a sunny lane
    Some boy and girl will meet and kiss and swear
        That nobody can love their way again
            While over there
    You will have smiled, I shall have tossed your hair.

## The Quiet House

WHEN we were children old Nurse used to say,
　　The house was like an auction or a fair
Until the lot of us were safe in bed.
It has been quiet as the country-side
Since Ted and Janey and then Mother died
And Tom crossed Father and was sent away.
After the lawsuit he could not hold up his head,
　　Poor Father, and he does not care
　　For people here, or to go anywhere.

To get away to Aunt's for that week-end
　　Was hard enough; (since then, a year ago,
　　He scarcely lets me slip out of his sight—)
At first I did not like my cousin's friend,
　　I did not think I should remember him:
　　His voice has gone, his face is growing dim
And if I like him now I do not know.
　　He frightened me before he smiled—
　　He did not ask me if he might—
　　He said that he would come one Sunday night,
　　He spoke to me as if I were a child.

No year has been like this that has just gone by;
　　It may be that what Father says is true,
If things are so it does not matter why:
　　But everything has burned, and not quite through.
　　The colours of the world have turned
　　To flame, the blue, the gold has burned
In what used to be such a leaden sky.
When you are burned quite through you die.

　　Red is the strangest pain to bear;
In Spring the leaves on the budding trees;
In Summer the roses are worse than these,
　　More terrible than they are sweet:
　　A rose can stab you across the street
　　　Deeper than any knife:
　　And the crimson haunts you everywhere—
Thin shafts of sunlight, like the ghosts of reddened swords have struck our sta
As if, coming down, you had spilt your life.

48

I think that my soul is red
Like the soul of a sword or a scarlet flower:
    But when these are dead
    They have had their hour.

    I shall have had mine, too,
        For from head to feet
    I am burned and stabbed half through,
        And the pain is deadly sweet.

    The things that kill us seem
        Blind to the death they give:
    It is only in our dream
        The things that kill us live.

The room is shut where Mother died,
    The other rooms are as they were,
The world goes on the same outside,
    The sparrows fly across the Square,
    The children play as we four did there,
    The trees grow green and brown and bare,
The sun shines on the dead Church spire,
    And nothing lives here but the fire.
While Father watches from his chair
            Day follows day
The same, or now and then a different grey,
            Till, like his hair,
Which Mother said was wavy once and bright,
            They will all turn white.

    To-night I heard a bell again—
Outside it was the same mist of fine rain,
The lamps just lighted down the long, dim street,
            No one for me—
    I think it is myself I go to meet:
I do not care; some day I *shall* not think; I shall not *be*

## The Forest Road

THE forest road,
   The infinite straight road stretching away
World without end: the breathless road between the walls
Of the black listening trees: the hushed, grey road
Beyond the window that you shut to-night
Crying that you would look at it by day—
There is a shadow there that sings and calls
But not for you. Oh! hidden eyes that plead in sleep
Against the lonely dark, if I could touch the fear
And leave it kissed away on quiet lids—
If I could hush these hands that are half-awake,
Groping for me in sleep I could go free.
I wish that God would take them out of mine
And fold them like the wings of frightened birds
Shot cruelly down, but fluttering into quietness so soon,
Broken, forgotten things; there is no grief for them in the green Spring
When the new birds fly back to the old trees.
But it shall not be so with you. I will look back. I wish I knew that God would stan
Smiling and looking down on you when morning comes,
To hold you, when you wake, closer than I,
So gently though: and not with famished lips or hungry arms:
He does not hurt the frailest, dearest things
As we do in the dark. See, dear, your hair—
I must unloose this hair that sleeps and dreams
About my face, and clings like the brown weed
To drowned, delivered things, tossed by the tired sea
Back to the beaches. Oh! your hair! If you had lain
A long time dead on the rough, glistening ledge
Of some black cliff, forgotten by the tide,
The raving winds would tear, the dripping brine would rust away
Fold after fold of all the loveliness
That wraps you round, and makes you, lying here,
The passionate fragrance that the roses are.
But death would spare the glory of your head
In the long sweetness of the hair that does not die:
The spray would leap to it in every storm,
The scent of the unsilenced sea would linger on
In these dark waves, and round the silence that was you—
Only the nesting gulls would hear—but there would still be whispers in your hair

Keep them for me; keep them for me. What *is* this singing on the road
That makes all other music like the music in a dream—
Dumb to the dancing and the marching feet; you know, in dreams, you see
Old pipers playing that you cannot hear,
And ghostly drums that only seem to beat. This seems to climb:
Is it the music of a larger place? It makes our room too small: it is like a stair,
A calling stair that climbs up to a smile you scarcely see,
Dim but so waited for; and *you* know what a smile is, how it calls,
How, if I smiled you always ran to me.
Now you must sleep forgetfully, as children do.
There is a Spirit sits by us in sleep
Nearer than those who walk with us in the bright day.
I think he has a tranquil, saving face: I think he came
Straight from the hills: he may have suffered there in time gone by,
And once, from those forsaken heights, looked down,
Lonely himself, on all the lonely sorrows of the earth.
It is his kingdom—Sleep. If I could leave you there—
If, without waking you, I could get up and reach the door—!
We used to go together.—Shut, scared eyes,
Poor, desolate, desperate hands, it is not I
Who thrust you off. No, take your hands away—
I cannot strike your lonely hands. Yes, I have struck your heart,
It did not come so near. Then lie you there
Dear and wild heart behind this quivering snow
With two red stains on it: and I will strike and tear
Mine out, and scatter it to yours. Oh! throbbing dust,
You that were life, our little wind-blown hearts!
                    The road! the road!
There is a shadow there: I see my soul,
I hear my soul, singing among the trees!


### On the Road to the Sea

WE passed each other, turned and stopped for half an hour, then went our way,
        I who make other women smile did not make you—
But no man can move mountains in a day.
        So this hard thing is yet to do.

But first I want your life:—before I die I want to see
   The world that lies behind the strangeness of your eyes,
There is nothing gay or green there for my gathering, it may be,
    Yet on brown fields there lies
A haunting purple bloom: is there not something in grey skies
     And in grey sea?
  I want what world there is behind your eyes,
  I want your life and you will not give it me.


  Now, if I look, I see you walking down the years,
  Young, and through August fields—a face, a thought, a swinging dream perched
   on a stile—;
  I would have liked (so vile we are!) to have taught you tears
    But most to have made you smile.


  To-day is not enough or yesterday: God sees it all—
Your length on sunny lawns, the wakeful rainy nights—; tell me—(how vain to ask
   but it is not a question—just a call—;
Show me then only your notched inches climbing up the garden wall,
    I like you best when you were small.


    Is this a stupid thing to say
    Not having spent with you one day?
  No matter; I shall never touch your hair
  Or hear the little tick behind your breast,
    Still it is there,
    And as a flying bird
  Brushes the branches where it may not rest
    I have brushed your hand and heard
  The child in you: I like that best.


So small, so dark, so sweet; and were you also then too grave and wise?
  Always I think. Then put your far off little hand in mine;—Oh! let it rest;
I will not stare into the early world beyond the opening eyes,
  Or vex or scare what I love best.
    But I want your life before mine bleeds away—
    Here—not in heavenly hereafters—soon,—
    I want your smile this very afternoon,
    (The last of all my vices, pleasant people used to say,
    I wanted and I sometimes got—the Moon!)

You know, at dusk, the last bird's cry,
And round the house the flap of the bat's low flight,
Trees that go black against the sky
And then—how soon the night!

No shadow of you on any bright road again,
And at the darkening end of this—what voice? whose kiss? As if you'd say!
It is not I who have walked with you, it will not be I who take away
Peace, peace, my little handful of the gleaner's grain
From your reaped fields at the shut of day.

Peace! Would you not rather die
Reeling,—with all the cannons at your ear?
So, at least, would I,
And I may not be here
To-night, to-morrow morning or next year.
Still I will let you keep your life a little while,
See dear?
*I have made you smile.*


## I Have Been Through the Gates

His heart, to me, was a place of palaces and pinnacles and shining towers;
I saw it then as we see things in dreams,—I do not remember how long I slept;
I remember the trees, and the high, white walls, and how the sun was always on the
    towers;
The walls are standing to-day, and the gates: I have been through the gates, I have
    groped, I have crept
Back, back. There is dust in the streets, and blood; they are empty; darkness is over
    them;
His heart is a place with the lights gone out, forsaken by great winds and the heavenly
    rain, unclean and unswept,
Like the heart of the holy city, old, blind, beautiful Jerusalem,
Over which Christ wept.

## The Road to Kerity

Do you remember the two old people we passed on the road to Kerity,
Resting their sack on the stones, by the drenched wayside,
Looking at us with their lightless eyes through the driving rain, and then out again
To the rocks, and the long white line of the tide:
Frozen ghosts that were children once, husband and wife, father and mother,
Looking at us with those frozen eyes; have you ever seen anything quite so chilled o
so old?

But we—with our arms about each other
We did not feel the cold!

## From a Window

Up here, with June, the sycamore throws
Across the window a whispering screen;
I shall miss the sycamore more, I suppose,
Than anything else on this earth that is out in green.
But I mean to go through the door without fear,
Not caring much what happens here
When I'm away:—
How green the screen is across the panes
Or who goes laughing along the lanes
With my old lover all the summer day.

## Not for that City

Not for that city of the level sun,
Its golden streets and glittering gates ablaze—
The shadeless, sleepless city of white days,
White nights, or nights and days that are as one—
We weary, when all is said, all thought, all done.

We strain our eyes beyond this dusk to see
What, from the threshold of eternity
We shall step into. No, I think we shun
The splendour of that everlasting glare,
  The clamour of that never-ending song.
  And if for anything we greatly long,
It is for some remote and quiet stair
    Which winds to silence and a space of sleep
    Too sound for waking and for dreams too deep.

### *Fin de Fête*

SWEETHEART, for such a day
    One mustn't grudge the score;
Here, then, it's all to pay,
    It's Good-night at the door.

Good-night and good dreams to you,—
    Do you remember the picture-book thieves
Who left two children sleeping in a wood the long night through,
    And how the birds came down and covered them with leaves?

So you and I should have slept,—But now,
    Oh, what a lonely head!
With just the shadow of a waving bough
    In the moonlight over your bed.

### *I so liked Spring*

I so liked Spring last year
    Because you were here;—
        The thrushes too—
Because it was these you so liked to hear—
        I so liked you.

55

This year's a different thing,—
I'll not think of you.
But I'll like Spring because it is simply Spring
As the thrushes do.

## Ne Me Tangito

"This man . . . would have known who and what manner of woman this is: for she a sinner."—*S. Luke* vii. 39.

ODD, *You* should fear the touch,
The first that I was ever ready to let go,
I, that have not cared much
For any toy I could not break and throw
To the four winds when I had done with it. You need not fear the touch,
Blindest of all the things that I have cared for very much
In the whole gay, unbearable, amazing show.

True—for a moment—no, dull heart, you were too small,
Thinking to hide the ugly doubt behind that hurried puzzled little smile:
Only the shade, was it, you saw? but still the shade of something vile:
Oddest of all!
So I will tell you this. Last night, in sleep,
Walking through April fields I heard the far-off bleat of sheep
And from the trees about the farm, not very high,
A flight of pigeons fluttered up into an early evening mackerel sky.
Someone stood by and it was you:
About us both a great wind blew.
My breast was bared
But sheltered by my hair
I found you, suddenly, lying there,
Tugging with tiny fingers at my heart, no more afraid:
The weakest thing, the most divine
That ever yet was mine,
Something that I had strangely made,
So then it seemed—
The child for which I had not looked or ever cared,
Of whom, before, I had never dreamed.

## My Heart is Lame

My heart is lame with running after yours so fast
      Such a long way,
Shall we walk slowly home, looking at all the things we passed
      Perhaps to-day?

Home down the quiet evening roads under the quiet skies,
      Not saying much,
You for a moment giving me your eyes
      When you could bear my touch.

But not to-morrow. This has taken all my breath;
      Then, though you look the same,
There may be something lovelier in Love's face in death
As your heart sees it, running back the way we came;
      *My* heart is lame.

## The Trees are Down

    —and he cried with a loud voice:
    Hurt not the earth, neither the sea, nor the trees—
             (Revelation.)

They are cutting down the great plane-trees at the end of the gardens.
    For days there has been the grate of the saw, the swish of the branches as they
    fall,
The crash of trunks, the rustle of trodden leaves,
With the "Whoops" and the "Whoas", the loud common talk, the loud common laughs
    of the men, above it all.

I remember one evening of a long past Spring
Turning in at a gate, getting out of a cart, and finding a large dead rat in the mud of
    the drive.
I remember thinking: alive or dead, a rat was a god-forsaken thing,
But at least, in May, that even a rat should be alive.

The week's work here is as good as done. There is just one bough
  On the roped bole, in the fine grey rain,
      Green and high
      And lonely against the sky.
        (Down now !—)
      And but for that,
      If an old dead rat
Did once, for a moment, unmake the Spring, I might never have thought of him again

It is not for a moment the Spring is unmade to-day;
These were great trees, it was in them from root to stem:
When the men with the "Whoops" and the "Whoas" have carted the whole of the
    whispering loveliness away
Half the Spring, for me, will have gone with them.

It is going now, and my heart has been struck with the hearts of the planes;
Half my life it has beat with these, in the sun, in the rains,
    In the March wind, the May breeze,
In the great gales that came over to them across the roofs from the great seas.
    There was only a quiet rain when they were dying;
    They must have heard the sparrows flying,
And the small creeping creatures in the earth where they were lying—
    But I, all day, I heard an angel crying:
      "Hurt not the trees".

## Absence

SOMETIMES I know the way
    You walk, up over the bay;
It is a wind from that far sea
That blows the fragrance of your hair to me.

Or in this garden when the breeze
    Touches my trees
To stir their dreaming shadows on the grass
    I see you pass.

In sheltered beds, the heart of every rose
    Serenely sleeps to-night. As shut as those
Your guarded heart; as safe as they from the beat, beat
Of hooves that tread dropped roses in the street.

    Turn never again
      On these eyes blind with a wild rain
    Your eyes; they were stars to me.—
      There are things stars may not see.

But call, call, and though Christ stands
    Still with scarred hands
Over my mouth, I must answer. So,
I will come—He shall let me go!


## Moorland Night

My face is against the grass—the moorland grass is wet—
    My eyes are shut against the grass, against my lips there are the little blades,
      Over my head the curlews call,
    And now there is the night wind in my hair;
My heart is against the grass and the sweet earth;—it has gone still, at last.
      It does not want to beat any more,
        And why should it beat?
    This is the end of the journey;
      The Thing is found.

      This is the end of all the roads—
    Over the grass there is the night-dew
And the wind that drives up from the sea along the moorland road;
    I hear a curlew start out from the heath
    And fly off, calling through the dusk,
      The wild, long, rippling call.
    The Thing is found and I am quiet with the earth.
Perhaps the earth will hold it, or the wind, or that bird's cry,
But it is not for long in any life I know. This cannot stay,
Not now, not yet, not in a dying world, with me, for very long.
      I leave it here:

And one day the wet grass may give it back—
One day the quiet earth may give it back—
The calling birds may give it back as they go by—
To someone walking on the moor who starves for love and will not know
Who gave it to all these to give away;
Or, if I come and ask for it again,
Oh! then, to me.

# DEATH AND BEYOND

## *Beside the Bed*

SOMEONE has shut the shining eyes, straightened and folded
    The wandering hands quietly covering the unquiet breast:
So, smoothed and silenced you lie, like a child not again to be questioned or scolded;
  But, for you, not one of us believes that this is rest.

Not so to close the windows down can cloud and deaden
  The blue beyond: or to screen the wavering flame subdue its breath:
Why, if I lay my cheek to your cheek, your grey lips, like dawn, would quiver and redden,
    Breaking into the old, odd smile at this fraud of death.

Because all night you have not turned to us or spoken
  It is time for you to wake; your dreams were never very deep:
I, for one, have seen the thin, bright, twisted threads of them dimmed suddenly and broken,
    This is only a most piteous pretence of sleep!

## *In Nunhead Cemetery*

IT is the clay that makes the earth stick to his spade;
    He fills in holes like this year after year;
The others have gone; they were tired, and half afraid,
    But I would rather be standing here;

There is nowhere else to go. I have seen this place
  From the windows of the train that's going past
Against the sky. This is rain on my face—
  It was raining here when I saw it last.

There is something horrible about a flower;
  This, broken in my hand, is one of those
He threw in just now: it will not live another hour;
  There are thousands more: you do not miss a rose.

One of the children hanging about
  Pointed at the whole dreadful heap and smiled
This morning, after THAT was carried out;
  There is something terrible about a child.

We were like children, last week, in the Strand;
  That was the day you laughed at me
Because I tried to make you understand
  The cheap, stale chap I used to be
  Before I saw the things you made me see.

This is not a real place; perhaps by-and-by
  I shall wake—I am getting drenched with all this rain:
To-morrow I will tell you about the eyes of the Crystal Palace train
  Looking down on us, and you will laugh and I shall see what you see agai̓

  Not here, not now. We said "Not yet
  Across our low stone parapet
Will the quick shadows of the sparrows fall".


## Exspecto Resurrectionem


OH! King Who hast the key
    Of that dark room,
The last which prisons us but held not Thee,
    Thou know'st its gloom.

Dost Thou a little love this one
    Shut in to-night,
Young and so piteously alone,
    Cold—out of sight?
Thou know'st how hard and bare
The pillow of that new-made narrow bed,
    Then leave not there
    So dear a head!


## Saturday Market

Bury your heart in some deep green hollow
    Or hide it up in a kind old tree;
Better still, give it the swallow
    When she goes over the sea.

In Saturday Market there's eggs a 'plenty
    And dead-alive ducks with their legs tied down,
Grey old gaffers and boys of twenty—
    Girls and the women of the town—
Pitchers and sugar-sticks, ribbons and laces,
    Posies and whips and dicky-birds' seed,
Silver pieces and smiling faces,
    In Saturday Market they've all they need.

What were you showing in Saturday Market
    That set it grinning from end to end
Girls and gaffers and boys of twenty—?
    Cover it close with your shawl, my friend—
Hasten you home with the laugh behind you,
    Over the down—, out of sight,
Fasten your door, though no one will find you,
    No one will look on a Market night.

See, you, the shawl is wet, take out from under
    The red dead thing—. In the white of the moon
On the flags does it stir again? Well, and no wonder!
    Best make an end of it; bury it soon.

If there is blood on the hearth who'll know it?
    Or blood on the stairs,
When a murder is over and done why show it?
    In Saturday Market nobody cares.

Then lie you straight on your bed for a short, short weeping
    And still, for a long, long rest,
There's never a one in the town so sure of sleeping
    As you, in the house on the down with a hole in your breast.

    Think no more of the swallow,
      Forget, you, the sea,
    Never again remember the deep green hollow
      Or the top of the kind old tree!

## *The Cenotaph*

### SEPTEMBER 1919

Not yet will those measureless fields be green again
    Where only yesterday the wild sweet blood of wonderful youth was shed;
There is a grave whose earth must hold too long, too deep a stain,
Though for ever over it we may speak as proudly as we may tread.
But here, where the watchers by lonely hearths from the thrust of an inward swo
    have more slowly bled,
We shall build the Cenotaph: Victory, winged, with Peace, winged too, at the colum
    head.
And over the stairway, at the foot—oh! here, leave desolate, passionate hands to spre
Violets, roses, and laurel, with the small, sweet, twinkling country things
Speaking so wistfully of other Springs,
From the little gardens of little places where son or sweetheart was born and bred.
In splendid sleep, with a thousand brothers
            To lovers—to mothers
            Here, too, lies he:
Under the purple, the green, the red,
It is all young life: it must break some women's hearts to see
Such a brave, gay coverlet to such a bed!
Only, when all is done and said,
God is not mocked and neither are the dead.

For this will stand in our Market-place—
Who'll sell, who'll buy
(Will you or I
Lie each to each with the better grace)?
While looking into every busy whore's and huckster's face
As they drive their bargains, is the Face
Of God: and some young, piteous, murdered face.

## Rooms

I REMEMBER rooms that have had their part
In the steady slowing down of the heart.
The room in Paris, the room at Geneva,
The little damp room with the seaweed smell,
And that ceaseless maddening sound of the tide—
Rooms where for good or for ill—things died.
But there is the room where we (two) lie dead,
Though every morning we seem to wake and might just as well seem to sleep again
As we shall somewhere in the other quieter, dustier bed
Out there in the sun—in the rain.

## Do Dreams Lie Deeper?

HIS dust looks up to the changing sky
Through daisies' eyes;
And when a swallow flies
Only so high
He hears her going by
As daisies do. He does not die
In this brown earth where he was glad enough to lie.

But looking up from that other bed,
"There is something more my own", he said,
"Than hands or feet or this restless head
That must be buried when I am dead.

E                                   65

The Trumpet may wake every other sleeper.
Do dreams lie deeper——?
And what sunrise
When these are shut shall open their little eyes?
They are my children, they have very lovely faces—
And how does one bury the breathless dreams?
They are not of the earth and not of the sea,
They have no friends here but the flakes of the falling snow;
You and I will go down two paces—
Where do they go?"

## Epitaph

H<small>E</small> loved gay things
        Yet with the brave
He laughed when he was covered with grey wings,
—Asking the darkest angel for bright things
        And the angel gave—
So with a smile he overstepped the grave.

## Friend, Wherefore——?

I <small>WILL</small> not count the years—there are days too—
        And to-night again I have said
    "What if you should be lying dead?"
Well, if it were so, I could only lay my head
        Quietly on the pillow of my bed
    Thinking of Him on whom poor sufferers cried
    Suffering Himself so much before He died:
    And then of Judas walking three years by His side—
    How Judas kissed Him—how He was crucified.
        Always when I see you
            I see those two;
        Oh! God it is true
    We do not, all of us, know what we do;
        But Judas knew.

# DEATH AND BEYOND

## Here Lies a Prisoner

LEAVE him: he's quiet enough: and what matter
     Out of his body or in, you can scatter
The frozen breath of his silenced soul, of his outraged soul to the winds that rave
Quieter now than he used to be, but listening still to the magpie chatter
     Over his grave.

## On Youth Struck Down

### (FROM AN UNFINISHED ELEGY)

OH! Death what have you to say?
     "Like a bride—like a bride-groom they ride away:
You shall go back to make up the fire,
To learn patience—to learn grief,
To learn sleep when the light has quite gone out of your earthly skies,
But they have the light in their eyes
     To the end of their day."

## Smile, Death

SMILE, Death, see I smile as I come to you
   Straight from the road and the moor that I leave behind,
Nothing on earth to me was like this wind-blown space,
Nothing was like the road, but at the end there was a vision or a face
    And the eyes were not always kind.

   Smile, Death, as you fasten the blades to my feet for me,
On, on let us skate past the sleeping willows dusted with snow;
Fast, fast down the frozen stream, with the moor and the road and the vision behind,
   (Show me your face, why the eyes are kind!)
And we will not speak of life or believe in it or remember it as we go.

# DEATH AND BEYOND
## *To a Child in Death*

You would have scoffed if we had told you yesterday
  Love made us feel, or so it was with me, like some great bird
   Trying to hold and shelter you in its strong wing;—
A gay little shadowy smile would have tossed us back such a solemn word,
   And it was not for that you were listening
   When so quietly you slipped away
With half the music of the world unheard.
What shall we do with this strange summer, meant for you,—
   Dear, if we see the winter through
   What shall be done with spring?
This, this is the victory of the Grave; here is death's sting,
That is not strong enough, our strongest wing.

But what of His who like a Father pitieth?
His Son was also, once, a little thing,
The wistfullest child that ever drew breath,
Chased by a sword from Bethlehem and in the busy house at Nazareth
Playing with little rows of nails, watching the carpenter's hammer swing,
Long years before His hands and feet were tied
And by a hammer and the three great nails He died,
   Of youth, of Spring,
Of sorrow, of loneliness, of victory the King,
   Under the shadow of that wing.

# MISCELLANEOUS

## *The Changeling*

Toll no bell for me, dear Father, dear Mother,
    Waste no sighs;
There are my sisters, there is my little brother
  Who plays in the place called Paradise,
Your children all, your children for ever;
        But I, so wild,
Your disgrace, with the queer brown face, was never,
  Never, I know, but half your child!

In the garden at play, all day, last summer,
      Far and away I heard
The sweet "tweet-tweet" of a strange new-comer,
  The dearest, clearest call of a bird.
It lived down there in the deep green hollow,
  My own old home, and the fairies say
The word of a bird is a thing to follow,
  So I was away a night and a day.

One evening, too, by the nursery fire,
  We snuggled close and sat round so still,
When suddenly as the wind blew higher,
  Something scratched on the window-sill.
A pinched brown face peered in—I shivered;
  No one listened or seemed to see;
The arms of it waved and the wings of it quivered,
  Whoo—I knew it had come for me;
  Some are as bad as bad can be!

All night long they danced in the rain,
Round and round in a dripping chain,
Threw their caps at the window-pane,
  Tried to make me scream and shout
  And fling the bedclothes all about:
I meant to stay in bed that night,
And if only you had left a light
  They would never have got me out.


Sometimes I wouldn't speak, you see,
  Or answer when you spoke to me,
Because in the long, still dusks of Spring
You can hear the whole world whispering:
  The shy green grasses making love,
  The feathers grow on the dear, grey dove,
  The tiny heart of the redstart beat,
  The patter of the squirrel's feet,
The pebbles pushing in the silver streams,
The rushes talking in their dreams,
  The swish-swish of the bat's black wings,
  The wild-wood bluebell's sweet ting-tings,
  Humming and hammering at your ear,
    Everything there is to hear
In the heart of hidden things,
  But not in the midst of the nursery riot.
  That's why I wanted to be quiet,
    Couldn't do my sums, or sing,
    Or settle down to anything.
  And when, for that, I was sent upstairs
  I *did* kneel down to say my prayers;
But the King who sits on your high church steeple
Has nothing to do with us fairy people!


'Times I pleased you, dear Father, dear Mother,
  Learned all my lessons and liked to play,
And dearly I loved the little pale brother
  Whom some other bird must have called away.
Why did They bring me here to make me
  Not quite bad and not quite good,
Why, unless They're wicked, do They want, in spite, to take me
  Back to their wet, wild wood?

Now, every night I shall see the windows shining,
　　The gold lamp's glow, and the fire's red gleam,
While the best of us are twining twigs and the rest of us are whining
　　In the hollow by the stream.
Black and chill are Their nights on the wold;
　　And They live so long and They feel no pain:
I shall grow up, but never grow old,
I shall always, always be very cold,
　　I shall never come back again!


## *Ken*


THE town is old and very steep,
　　A place of bells and cloisters and grey towers,
And black-clad people walking in their sleep—
　　A nun, a priest, a woman taking flowers
　　To her new grave; and watched from end to end
　　By the great Church above, through the still hours:
　　　But in the morning and the early dark
The children wake to dart from doors and call
Down the wide, crooked street, where, at the bend,
　　Before it climbs up to the park,
Ken's is the gabled house facing the Castle wall.

When first I came upon him there
Suddenly, on the half-lit stair,
I think I hardly found a trace
Of likeness to a human face
　　In his. And I said then
If in His image God made men,
Some other must have made poor Ken—
But for his eyes which looked at you
As two red, wounded stars might do.

He scarcely spoke, you scarcely heard,
His voice broke off in little jars
To tears sometimes. An uncouth bird

He seemed as he ploughed up the street,
Groping, with knarred, high-lifted feet
And arms thrust out as if to beat
    Always against a threat of bars.


And oftener than not there'd be
A child just higher than his knee
Trotting beside him. Through his dim
    Long twilight this, at least, shone clear,
    That all the children and the deer,
      Whom every day he went to see
Out in the park, belonged to him.


    "God help the folk that next him sits
    He fidgets so, with his poor wits,"
The neighbours said on Sunday nights
When he would go to Church to "see the lights!"
    Although for these he used to fix
    His eyes upon a crucifix
    In a dark corner, staring on
    Till everybody else had gone.
    And sometimes, in his evil fits,
You could not move him from his chair—
You did not look at him as he sat there,
    Biting his rosary to bits.
While pointing to the Christ he tried to say
    "Take it away".


    Nothing was dead:
He said "a bird" if he picked up a broken wing,
    A perished leaf or any such thing
    Was just "a rose"; and once when I had said
He must not stand and knock there any more,
He left a twig on the mat outside my door.


    Not long ago
The last thrush stiffened in the snow,
    While black against a sullen sky
    The sighing pines stood by.

But now the wind has left our rattled pane
To flutter the hedge-sparrow's wing,
The birches in the wood are red again
    And only yesterday
The larks went up a little way to sing
    What lovers say
  Who loiter in the lanes to-day;
  The buds begin to talk of May
With learned rooks on city trees,
    And if God please
    With all of these
We, too, shall see another Spring.


But in that red brick barn upon the hill
  I wonder——can one own the deer,
And does one walk with children still
    As one did here?
    Do roses grow
Beneath those twenty windows in a row—
    And if some night
When you have not seen any light
They cannot move you from your chair
    What happens there?
    I do not know.


  So, when they took
Ken to that place, I did not look
After he called and turned on me
His eyes. These I shall see—


## On the Asylum Road

THEIRS is the house whose windows—every pane—
  Are made of darkly stained or clouded glass:
Sometimes you come upon them in the lane,
  The saddest crowd that you will ever pass.

But still we merry town or village folk
    Throw to their scattered stare a kindly grin,
And think no shame to stop and crack a joke
    With the incarnate wages of man's sin.

None but ourselves in our long gallery we meet.
    The moor-hen stepping from her reeds with dainty feet,
      The hare-bell bowing on his stem,
Dance not with us; their pulses beat
    To fainter music; nor do we to them
      Make their life sweet.

The gayest crowd that they will ever pass
    Are we to brother-shadows in the lane:
Our windows, too, are clouded glass
    To them, yes, every pane!

## The Sunlit House

WHITE through the gate it gleamed and slept
    In shuttered sunshine: the parched garden flowers,
Their fallen petals from the beds unswept,
    Like children unloved and ill-kept
      Dreamed through the hours.
Two blue hydrangeas by the blistered door, burned brown.
    Watched there and no one in the town
    Cared to go past it night or day,
    Though why this was they wouldn't say.
But I, the stranger, knew that I must stay,
    Pace up the weed-grown paths and down,
    Till one afternoon—there is just a doubt—
    But I fancy I heard a tiny shout—
    From an upper window a bird flew out—
      And I went my way.

## The Shade-Catchers

I THINK they were about as high
 As haycocks are. They went running by
Catching bits of shade in the sunny street:
"I've got one", cried sister to brother.
 "I've got two." "Now I've got another."
But scudding away on their little bare feet,
They left the shade in the sunny street.

## Love Love To-day

LOVE love to-day, my dear,
 Love is not always here;
Wise maids know how soon grows sere
 The greenest leaf of Spring;
 But no man knoweth
 Whither it goeth
 When the wind bloweth
 So frail a thing.

Love love, my dear, to-day,
 If the ship's in the bay,
If the bird has come your way
 That sings on summer trees;
 When his song faileth
 And the ship saileth
 No voice availeth
 To call back these.

## Domus Caedet Arborem

EVER since the great planes were murdered at the end of the gardens
 The city, to me, at night has the look of a Spirit brooding crime;
As if the dark houses watching the trees from dark windows
 Were simply biding their time.

*Again*

ONE day, not here, you will find a hand
    Stretched out to you as you walk down some heavenly street;
You will see a stranger scarred from head to feet;
But when he speaks to you you will not understand,
Nor yet who wounded him nor why his wounds are sweet.
    And saying nothing, letting go his hand,
    You will leave him in the heavenly street—
      So we shall meet!

*May*, 1915

LET us remember Spring will come again
    To the scorched, blackened woods, where the wounded trees
Wait with their old wise patience for the heavenly rain,
Sure of the sky: sure of the sea to send its healing breeze,
    Sure of the sun. And even as to these
      Surely the Spring, when God shall please,
    Will come again like a divine surprise
To those who sit to-day with their great Dead, hands in their hands, eyes in their eye
At one with Love, at one with Grief: blind to the scattered things and changing skie

*June*, 1915

WHO thinks of June's first rose to-day?
    Only some child, perhaps, with shining eyes and rough bright hair will reac
      it down
In a green sunny lane, to us almost as far away
    As are the fearless stars from these veiled lamps of town.
    What's little June to a great broken world with eyes gone dim
    From too much looking on the face of grief, the face of dread?
      Or what's the broken world to June and him
    Of the small eager hand, the shining eyes, the rough bright head?

## The Rambling Sailor

Iɴ the old back streets o' Pimlico,
On the docks at Monte Video,
At the Ring o' Bells on Plymouth Hoe
He'm arter me now wheerever I go.
An' dirty nights when the wind do blow
I can hear him sing-songin' up from sea:
Oh! no man nor woman's bin friend to me
An' to-day I'm feared wheer to-morrow I'll be,
Sin' the night the moon lay whist and white
On the road goin' down to the Lizard Light
When I heard him hummin' behind me.

*"Oh! look, boy, look in your sweetheart's eyes*
  *So deep as sea an' so blue as skies;*
*An' 'tis better to kiss than to chide her.*
*If they tell 'ee no tales, they'll tell 'ee no lies*
    *Of the little brown mouse*
    *That creeps into the house*
*To lie sleepin' so quiet beside her.*

*"Oh! hold 'ee long, but hold 'ee light*
*Your true man's hand when you find him,*
*He'll help 'ee home on a darksome night*
    *Wi' a somethin' bright*
    *That he'm holdin' tight*
*In the hand that he keeps behind him.*

*"Oh! sit 'ee down to your whack o' pies,*
*So hot's the stew and the brew likewise,*
*But whiles you'm scrapin' the plates and dishes,*
  *A'gapin' down in the shiversome sea*
  *For the delicate mossels inside o' we*
*Theer's a passel o' hungry fishes."*

At the *Halte des Marins* at *Saint Nazaire*
I cussed him, sittin' astride his chair;
An' Christmas Eve on the Mary Clare
I pitched him a'down the hatch-way stair.

But "Shoutin' and cloutin's nothing to me,
Nor the hop nor the skip nor the jump", says he,
"For I be walkin' on every quay—"

*"So look, boy, look in the dear maid's eyes*
*And take the true man's hand*
*And eat your fill o' your whack o' pies*
*Till you'm starin' up wheer the sea-crow flies*
*Wi' your head lyin' soft in the sand."*

## The Call

FROM our low seat beside the fire
     Where we have dozed and dreamed and watched
          the glow
Or raked the ashes, stopping so
We scarcely saw the sun or rain
Above, or looked much higher
Than this same quiet red or burned-out fire,
     To-night we heard a call,
     A rattle on the window-pane,
     A voice on the sharp air,
And felt a breath stirring our hair,
     A flame within us: Something swift and tall
Swept in and out and that was all.
Was it a bright or a dark angel? Who can know?
     It left no mark upon the snow,
          But suddenly it snapped the chain,
          Unbarred, flung wide the door
          Which will not shut again;
And so we cannot sit here any more.
          We must arise and go:
          The world is cold without
          And dark and hedged about
          With mystery and enmity and doubt,
               But we must go
          Though yet we do not know
Who called, or what marks we shall leave upon the snow.

# INDEX OF FIRST LINES

*80306*

# INDEX OF FIRST LINES

*Poems so marked were included in the second edition of *The Farmer's Bride* (Poetry Bookshop, 1921). The rest were published posthumously in *The Rambling Sailor* (Poetry Bookshop, 1929).